Blooms *and* the Bard
Painted Sonnets

Angela Bell Julien

Blooms and the Bard: Painted Sonnets

Published by Wheatmark®
1760 East River Road, Suite 145
Tucson, Arizona 85718
U.S.A.
www.wheatmark.com

ISBN: 978-1-60494-920-9 (paperback)
ISBN: 978-1-60494-921-6 (ebook)
LCCN: 2012955294

rev201301

I would like to dedicate this book to my parents, George H. Bell, Jr. and Frankie Laverne Hawkins. These two very left-brained, mathematical people nurtured a very right-brained verbal child and encouraged me to be my own person. My mother taught me to be strong, to see the beauty in others, and to complete my journeys. My father inspired me to believe that I could always swim to shore no matter how far out in the lake we were when the boat sank. Optimism is a mighty gift.

Thank you to Jacob Chinn, *Jacob Chinn Photography*, for photographing my paintings.

Contents

Foreword

I've prepared to write *Blooms and the Bard: Painted Sonnets* for as long as I can remember. Sketching flowers helped me through every phase of life. I hope my teachers will forgive the fields of flowers sketched in class when I was supposed to be taking notes. As a child my parents would take me for rides through miles of flower fields just south of Phoenix. I could never get enough of looking at them. After many enjoyable years as a literature and writing teacher, I took on a fairly stressful job, principal of an urban high school. My husband knew the importance of flowers in my life and had a fresh bouquet sent to my office every Monday morning. I would often stare at them for inspiration. They were speaking to me; it just took me years to figure out what they were saying.

Similarly, I read almost everything Shakespeare wrote, engrossed in every line. I realized sometime later that what I really learned from the greatest bard was a love of language—of syntax and sound and double meanings. He wrote making use of rhyme and rhythm to give the readers a melodic symphony of words. But more importantly, Shakespeare played with language. Occasionally the rhyme would slightly miss, or jump a beat. He was having fun, making a point or teasing the reader-listener. What Shakespeare wrote was meant to be seen and heard.

So it is with *Blooms and the Bard: Painted Sonnets.* I hope you will read the sonnets aloud, with others, and enjoy the language, double meanings, and imagery. I know some of the words are not often used, or I have used them in an unusual fashion, so on the page after each sonnet I have given some definition to them. Some readers have told me the fun is in figuring out the meanings; if that is how you feel, don't read the page following the sonnet! Although all of the sonnets were inspired by someone or several someones, they are not intended to describe any specific person. You may know some pinks, or oranges, or blues, but probably most of us are hybrids. Some of us may even be hiding our inner red!

The paintings, too, are intentionally not any specific flower. If they resemble a flower you know, it is purely coincidental! They are intended only to give the essence of the flower, to make you think of flowers you have known.

Trying to decide on the order of the sonnets caused me much consternation. I finally just went with what made sense to me. You can read them in any order you like. I hope you enjoy them and then make use of the page that follows to write your own impressions about the oranges, blues, purples in your life. As a teacher I often needed to think about specific students and find their positive attributes. So often we begin with what bothers us about others; these sonnets take the opposite approach. Looking for the internal worth of individuals builds an understanding of ourselves and our perceptions of the world.

In case you are new to sonnets, they are generally fourteen lines of iambic pentameter. If English class is long ago and far away, that means each line is ten syllables with the accent on every other syllable beginning with the second syllable. If you just read them as you would any piece of text, following the punctuation, they will flow easily.

Sonnets also follow a regular rhyme pattern. You will see that I used a few different patterns ... just because it is more fun that way.

Sometimes there is a "twist" either after the eighth or twelfth line. Sometimes not.

Thank you for picking up *Blooms and the Bard: Painted Sonnets*. I hope you enjoy reading and talking about the sonnets as much as I enjoyed writing and painting them!

Green

Green

The bud of potent possibility
Is Green. The seed sends life to fill the air,
To meet the sky and find propinquity
With God, with grace—with strength enough to bear
The wind, the rain, the pain of human kind.
Green turns the branch from bare to beauty bold;
It tells of change, of hope, of love to bind
The warmth of spring and out the winter's cold.

With green, the earth and man survive to tell
Of times before the colors came to be
As one. Of how the people's fate befell
Not tragedy, but harmony. We see

'tis Green whose work has set our world apart,
To be a place of justice, peace and heart.

Special words—used creatively or for their interesting sounds or meanings:

Propinquity (pronounced pro-pink-witty) is one of my very favorite words. It means closeness—either physically, mentally or spiritually: a kinship. It is a perfect word for greens and their relationship with beauty.

Befell sort of means "happened to" but here it has a stronger meaning that includes fate. It is a much more interesting word and it makes the syllables work in the sonnet.

Justice is an often misused word. Here I use my favorite meaning of the word which is "righteousness."

Green people earn my respect and admiration.

Greens that I have known . . .

_____

_____

_____

_____

_____

_____

_____

_____

_____

_____

_____

_____

White

White

In light, white combines the colors all;
But garden's white is pallet for the rest—
A budding future, unmarked by weather's test.
An unembellished frame of canvas calls
Upon the brush to touch the sheet and cast
A hue to brighten both—to give, to serve
As partner to the deeper tints' contrast
And yet the purity of both preserve.

Our eyes are unaccustomed to the sight
Of simple wonders, natural gifts of art.
—So deputy of beauty, white, imparts
Look here! See here! Behold the streaming light!

Plain white prepares the portrait of the earth
Exquisitely providing color's birth.

Special words—used creatively or for their interesting sounds or meanings:

Unembellished sometimes just means "plain," but my meaning is "modest."

Deputy I know this seems like a simple word, but I love the word and all of its possible connotations in this sonnet, including helper, sidekick, protector, and official.

I didn't know until I became involved in stage lighting, that if you combine streams of light of all the colors, they become white. The fact still fascinates me. I must have been drawing flowers in science class when we covered light rays.

I appreciate the White flowers who have helped me bloom.

Deputies of beauty . . .

_____

_____

_____

_____

_____

_____

_____

_____

_____

_____

_____

Orange

Orange

The orange blossom bursts upon the scene
To stir the eye and wake the soul serene.
Though many try to only glance, the hue
Enrapts, engulfs, beguiles the whole milieu.
Mixed red of fire and yellow's sunlit sheen
Pure joy, illuminates a swathed wide screen,
Performing grandly for the florist right on cue
—As though announcing loudly life's debut.

The showy bloom's a pleaser to the crowd,
Vivacious, vibrant, value so endowed
That others often feel pastel compared.
The brilliant color's tint just must be shared.

But is the orange petal really keen,
Or only a beloved drama queen?

Special words—used creatively or for their interesting sounds or meanings:

Enrapts is a word you won't find in the dictionary. It is a shortened version of *enraptures,* which means to fill with delight. So enrapts would be a verb that would mean to make delightful.

Beguiles means to charm or trick.

Milieu is another one of my favorite words. It's origin is French and it means a social environment. I don't think there is an English equivalent.

Keen was a very popular slang term at one time, used to mean "cool" or popular. The slang meaning has crept its way into regular usage. It is a great little word with rich meaning.

Orange people make my life rich.

Orange people . . .

_____

_____

_____

_____

_____

_____

_____

_____

_____

_____

_____

Blue

Blue

With solid strength of petals bloomed supine,
The stock of blue holds steady in the wind.
Reflecting sky and water's sunlit shine,
A sense of immortality is penned.
Imbued by oceans everlasting tides
And juxtaposed with heaven's untold tales,
Blue seeks to fill the field and danger chides.
Unheeding harsh terrains, the plume prevails.

In Spring the ink of blue will dot the land,
Then with a summer breeze the stain will wax
With potent liberty and license grand—
'Til Autumn blots the legend's fierce climax

And Winter tames Blue's page to read
—Has left the seeds for rain and air to breed.

Special words—used creatively or for their interesting sounds or meanings:

Supine is the position of lying on your back with your face upwards or having outstretched hands with palms upward. I see it as someone enjoying the greatness of their place in the world.

Imbued is when someone is impregnated or inspired or as in this sonnet, both.

Juxtaposed—I love the sound of this word. It is when two or more things are compared by being "posed" next to one another.

Wax—In the sonnet, the word means spreading out, overtaking, increasing in size.

Potent is powerful, influential, virile.

License is used in the sonnet as in "artistic license," for dramatic effect, in a grand fashion.

Blue people write their own stories and intrigue me.

Blues make me . . .

_____

_____

_____

_____

_____

_____

_____

_____

_____

_____

_____

Red

Red

Beware of red. The floral designee
Of heat. Impassioned senses summon thee
—Perfume impossible to cast aside.
A scarlet guise allows a thorn to hide.
In red resides emotion raw and pure,
Oblivious of an inborn allure.
Beware of red. Ignore to no avail—
Embrace and risk the bramble's sharp impale.

Beware of red; but do not turn away
Lean close, breathe in, and all fears will allay.
The sharp beneath the soft keeps red unharmed.
Within the bed of blooms red's life is charmed.

Love red for both the tack and velvet weave
Red's truth in better and in worse, believe.

Special words—used creatively or for their interesting sounds or meanings:

Guise, as in the *second* half of *disguise*, a mask or cover.

Allay means to take away, lessen especially when it comes to fear.

I think the rest of the words are fairly clear— but Reds are complicated people. Maybe red is the complicated part of all of us.

Oh, the Red in me . . .

_____

_____

_____

_____

_____

_____

_____

_____

_____

_____

_____

Purple

Purple

When purple punches playfully from the ground
Impertinent, irreverent —a jest—
The posy patch reveals its favorite clown,
A robust humor born of nature's breast
So rich in whimsy; prickly to the touch.
The others dance to purple's breezy tone.
A wild and crazy step, a jig with such
Amusing beat—the blossom stands alone.

To somber souls, the violet sprout's display
May be too ticklish, too unbound, too free
Capricious, silly, challenging their grey,
They do not see the need for revelry.

But purple makes life's window box a gem;
It is from whence the spirit's laughter stems.

Special words—used creatively or for their interesting sounds or meanings:

Impertinent is lacking the sort of respect some people think is appropriate but is often humorous to those who are not expecting the respect.

Irreverent is when someone is satiric, flippant, not taking things that other people consider serious, seriously.

Capricious people are whimsical and unpredictable. I almost named my older daughter "Caprice." She is glad I didn't, although it would have fit her.

Revelry is that noisy fun often associated with spring break!

Purples give me the greatest gift—laughter!

Purples . . .

_____

_____

_____

_____

_____

_____

_____

_____

_____

_____

_____

_____

Yellow

Yellow

Ah, yellow, the eternal optimist,
With tickled morning light, the meadow paints
—Then giggles like a baby just been kissed.
For yellow, life's to live without restraint.
From seeds so full of mirthful merriment,
To laughter deep within, is yellow's mark.
An animated grin so confident—
The affirmation of a warming spark.

But growing wild is not always carefree;
The smile that yellow fondly dons belies
A strength to find the joy where others see
Nothing but pitfalls which their patience tries

Ah, yellow, blooms with faithful spirit light
To feel the mud of life—and find delight!

Special words—used creatively or for their interesting sounds or meanings:

Mirthful, those wonderful moments when people feel happy in an innocent, naïve sort of way.

I want to know more Yellows—they are the ones who keep me calm.

Yellows help me . . .

_____

_____

_____

_____

_____

_____

_____

_____

_____

_____

_____

_____

Pink

Pink

So innocent, so sweet the petal pink,
Tiny blossoms fragile to the touch.
An heirloom of the past not asking much,
A breath of air, a warm caress, and drink
Of morning's dew. A tiny tat of lace;
The fragrance of the mist just after rain.
A blush that tinges cheeks across the plains.
The legacy left from a time of grace.

But wait, the petals pink may muster might
When need prevails and weaker souls cry out.
The dignity of pink's assembled clout
Creates a flur of fighting for the right.

So pink presents a paradox on earth
From soft, is tempered power given birth.

Special words—used creatively or for their interesting sounds or meanings:

Tat is a small, delicate knot used to form lace. When you put several "tats" together it forms that beautiful lacey design that is actually quite strong.

Flur—I used a shortened form of flurry—but I like it to mean a huge gathering.

Paradox is a statement that seems contradictory—but in the long run makes sense—yet another of my favorite words.

Pinks make the world a warm and safe place for me.

Pinks . . .

_____

_____

_____

_____

_____

_____

_____

_____

_____

_____

_____

.

Gold

Gold

The golden blossoms guild the flower patch
With grace and style; gold radiates a glow,
An elegance—somewhat aloof—detached,
Yet charming, generous, the one to know.
A spicy scent bespeaks an inner air
Of poise and confidence. A champagne taste,
A classic core of strength with fancy flair.
A complicated mix of wild and chaste.

Gold emanates a fragrance boldly born
Of powdered pollen carried in the air
Invisible; gold permeates the morn
—An ambrosial perfume of heaven's care.

To earth a gift of value unbeknown
Much like the element of precious stone.

Special words—used creatively or for their interesting sounds or meanings:

Guild is that beautiful process of covering something with gold and making it look shiny, rich and beautiful.

Bespeaks is telling without talking—just making it clear.

Chaste, a lovely word used to mean pure, virgin.

Ambrosial—I use it to mean both a sweet mixture and heavenly.

Golds mystify me; I love to try to get close to them.

Solid Golds . . .

_____

_____

_____

_____

_____

_____

_____

_____

_____

_____

_____

The
Bouquet

The Bouquet

Each flower holds a beauty of its own
A wave—an independent stream of light
But when the rays are gathered up, not sown
Alone, bound waves design an image bright.
A sight as stunning to the eye as fine
Liqueur is to the tongue, exhilarating
And smooth, allowing senses to combine.
—A flowery cocktail—intoxicating

The breathtaking bouquet inebriates,
Unfolds the mind—lets go long held restraints
The synergy of colors merged creates
A palette rife with nature's paints.

That is, a bunch of flowers simply told.
Can hold the mystic message of the soul.

Special words—used creatively or for their interesting sounds or meanings:

Synergy, the last of my favorite words, means coming together to create something better, working together smoothly.

Rife means full of, plenty, overflowing.

Liqueur—my favorite is Bailey's Irish Crème, so smooth and soft and warm when I drink it.

My greatest hope is that someday, we will all appreciate what others bring to the bouquet.

The Bouquet of my life . . .

_____

_____

_____

_____

_____

_____

_____

_____

_____

_____

_____

CPSIA information can be obtained
at www.ICGtesting.com
Printed in the USA
BVIC010313170413
318382BV00001B